Ponies

by Diana Noonan

SCHOOL PUBLISHERS

Cover ©Getty; 3 ©Getty; 4 ©Telescope; 5 ©Photodisc; 6–7 ©Photolibrary.com; 8 ©Telescope; 9 ©Rob Cruse; 10 ©Getty; 11 ©Photolibrary.com; 12 ©ANT Photo Library; 13–14 ©Photolibrary.com.

Printed in Mexico

ISBN 10: 0-15-350637-7
ISBN 13: 978-0-15-350637-6

Ordering Options
ISBN 10: 0-15-350599-0 (Grade 2 On-Level Collection)
ISBN 13: 978-0-15-350599-7 (Grade 2 On-Level Collection)
ISBN 10: 0-15-357814-9 (package of 5)
ISBN 13: 978-0-15-357814-4 (package of 5)

3 4 5 6 7 8 9 10   050   15 14 13 12 11 10 09 08

What Is My Pet?

I live on a small farm. I have
a pony called Patches. Some ponies
are as small as a large dog. My pony
is larger than my bicycle. She is just
the right size for me to ride.

What Are Ponies?

Ponies are mammals. Mother mammals make milk for their babies. Baby ponies are called foals.

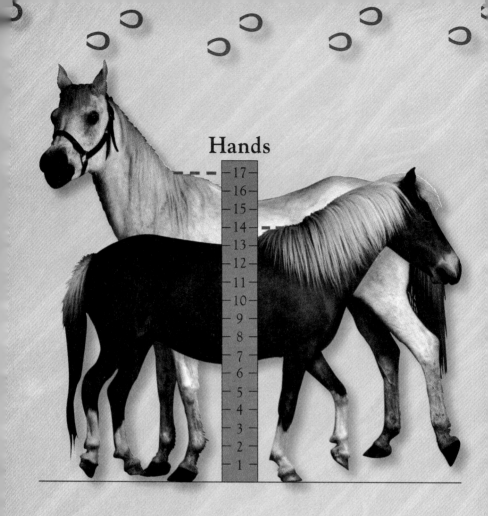

Hands

17
16
15
14
13
12
11
10
9
8
7
6
5
4
3
2
1

Ponies are small horses. People
are measured in feet. Horses are
measured in hands. Ponies can
be up to fourteen hands tall.

Where Does My Pony Live?

My pony lives in a large field. At night, she stays in a stable. There is food and water in the stable.

What Does My Pony Eat?

Ponies like to eat fresh grass. They also like to eat hay, a dried grass. For a special treat, my pony gets a sugar cube. She likes apples, too.

Things My Pony Needs

My pony needs a safe place to live. Our field has strong fences and some trees. In the summer, the shade from the trees keeps my pony cool.

In the winter, my pony needs
a warm blanket. She wears the
blanket in the field when it is cold.
She goes into the stable when the
weather is bad.

Ponies need special shoes for their feet, or hooves. Each shoe is shaped like a "U." The shoes protect the hooves.

What Do I Do for My Pony?

I brush my pony's coat every day. I always check that she is walking right. I give her food and fresh water.

I ride my pony as often as I can.
Riding gives my pony exercise.
It helps her to stay healthy.

It is also good exercise for me.
I teach my pony tricks. She can
jump over some rails.

What Can My Pony Do?

My pony can take me for rides.
She can go to the pony show with me.

We sometimes win a prize!

Think Critically

1. What is something that mother mammals do for their babies?

2. What are some facts you learned about ponies from this book?

3. What do all people who own ponies need to do for them?

4. What could happen if a pony didn't have shoes?

5. Would you like to have a pony? Why or why not?

 Science

Make a Poster Make a poster called *Taking Care of Pets*. List all the things that pet owners should do for their animals.

School-Home Connection Share this book with a family member. Talk about how a pony is like and different from other kinds of pets.

Word Count: 320 (321 with words in graphic)